American Linden

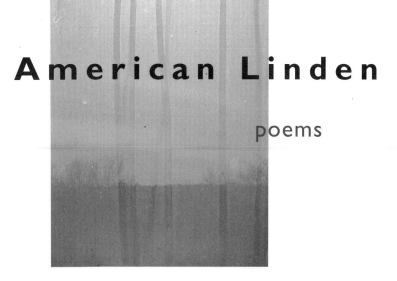

American Linden

poems

Matthew Zapruder

TUPELO PRESS

Dorset, Vermont

American Linden
Copyright © 2002 Matthew Zapruder
Printed in Canada

First paperback edition, 2002
ISBN 0-9710310-9-6
Library of Congress Control Number: 2002111993

First hardcover edition, 2002
ISBN 1-932195-05-X

Tupelo Press
PO Box 539, Dorset, Vermont 05251
802.366.8185 • Fax 802.362.1883
editor@tupelopress.org • web www.tupelopress.org

Cover and author photograph by J. Johnson
Cover and text designed by William Kuch, WK Graphic Design

American Linden

Winner of the Tupelo Press
Editors' Prize for Poetry

ACKNOWLEDGMENTS

Thanks to the editors of the following journals, where poems in this book (sometimes with different titles) first appeared: BARROW STREET, BOSTON REVIEW, BOTH, CONDUIT, CORDITE (Australia), CROWD, DUCKY, FENCE, HARVARD REVIEW, ISLAND (Australia), JUBILAT, LIT, NC2, THE NEW YORKER, QUARTERLY WEST, SALT (UK), SLOPE, WILLIAM AND MARY REVIEW, VERSE, VOLT.

Whoever You Are was featured on the website Poetry Daily (www.poems.com) on July 2nd, 2000, and was nominated for a Pushcart Prize.

The Book of Paintings appeared in THE FIFTH QUESTION AND AFTER: POEMS FOR TOMAZ SALAMUN, edited by Kevin Hart, Vagabond Press, Sydney, 2001.

The Book of Leaves and *What Exists* appeared in Slovenian and English in DAYS OF POETRY AND WINE, Medana, 2001.

I would like to extend great thanks to the following people: my parents and brother and sister; my friends; my teachers; and especially Dara, Jim, Peter, Brian, Matt and Joshua, without whom this book would never have been written.

CONTENTS

1–   Sweet Jesus

3–   The Artist Must Incline His Head Just So

4–   I Go Out to Meet Them

6–   Whoever You Are

8–   Sometimes Leaving

10–   Blueprint

11–   Before the Poem

12–   Mind the Gap

13–   View Onto the Balcony

14–   Summer Camp

16–   Park Slope

18–   A Colossal Historical Blunder

19–   September First

21–   The Invisible City of Kitezh

22–   The Path to the Orchard

23–   Coda

27–   The Book of Leaves

30–   Cupola

32–   Lean To

34–   The Blue Lights

35–   Tiburon

36–   The Book of Paintings

38–   New Haven

39–   A Return

40–   School Street

43–   What Exists

44– A History of Petersburg

45– The House Across the Water

46– Not Me, Not You

49– Spring

50– Kick the Can

52– Arcadia

53– The Book of Oakland

54– Friends of Olivia

57– These Windows

58– Warning: Sad

60– The Book of the Old World

61– Do You Remember

62– Scarecrow

63– The Book of Waves

65– American Linden

66– The Book of the Broken Window

69– I Am a Sculptor

71– Ten Questions for Mona

73– I Have a Friend

75– So Be It

77– The Book of the Wrong Kind of Blue

SWEET JESUS

Tea, tea, butter, the structure.
We were discussing the death
of iambic pentameter,
though we didn't know it.
She said with the notch
above her lips
I have a perfect ass
and I thought the thing about asses
is they're not perfect,
they have a kind of fatal flaw,
but I wasn't going to argue
with such a proud collection
of stumbling convergences.
I wanted to say, can I stick
my eyes down your throat?
but what emerged
was those eyebrows,
are they for rent?
How are they tragic?
By announcing a mountainlessness
that aches for its climbers,
a brow that needs
no announcing,
lips that shift
as mapped by insomnia,
one hidden rippling
bone that can never.
A patio floated by.
About us a Cambridge was revolving.
Somewhere marriage was discussing
a couple flattened
by the new gravity of summer,

but it wasn't us, we were refusing
to cross that most glorious
breed of slowness.
I vow I will touch you
always more distant stranger.

THE ARTIST MUST INCLINE HIS HEAD JUST SO

Often I have an idea and say it immediately.
If people praise me I wear the world
shyly on top of my head.
At times I'm compelled
like a fever to float
without any distinctions,
a sea of tin cans, love letters and greed.
The world is good for my pleasure and consumption.
I admire it totally, it stands
like a mountain inside and outside me.
Some art may be good, some dishonest.
There's no pressing need for conscription or liberty,
though a carful of people rides down the highway
too fast, clouded in song.
My lack of compassion astounds me,
and must not come to know itself.   –3–
It's true, I've never done anything
quite like striking you across the face.
There is of course the question of fate,
and whether it can be angered.
Example: when not overpowered by grief
there are proper and improper ways to mourn.
In such cases my gestures are shadows
cast far from myself
by one who crawls through the library,
touching the books that she touched.
I have dream after dream and forget each one.

I GO OUT TO MEET THEM

Terrible flowerbox
on my shoulders
unbuilt by the gold claws
logic and lightning,
speak the last word,
rewrite me. Dead bird
passing me like a friend,
dead bird frozen
in snow I was frozen
in happiness you're so beautiful.
With tiny golden claws you built
the painted book
of afternoon
afternoon stared into.
You said the world must have a border.
You renounced the borderless world.
You said the world
must have two claws,
one frozen in happiness,
one lit with gold laughter
past me gliding,
a bicycle under a friend.
A man coughs
therefore
the end of the world.
Therefore down alleys
that do not yet exist
I resolve to greet
each person more sadly.
To put music
back in a drawer.
To remove it

only when it needs me.
What kind of music
pins my sleep
with gold thread among the elms?
Blossoms die
in my hand as I prune them,
you can't win election,
you can't prosecute night
though we all heard it chuckling
idea of love.
Idea of love
in a white dress bewildered,
I'd prefer each friday
not be so sundown.
I'd prefer my memory
dizzy from dancing
for the memory
of dancing for soldiers.
Light and wind
put me down in this room.
Night has only one use for me.
Branches come closer,
bringing snow to my bedside.
The chairlift
how to remember mounts up
to a lake
nobody
knew in the stars.

WHOEVER YOU ARE

As the wayward satellite believes its rescuers
will come with white and weightless hands,
and the rescuers turning and floating believe
in their tethers and all those uninspected latches,
as madness believes in the organizing principle,
and allows it to strap her down on the gurney,
and the tiny island believes the sound
of a harp will arrive on the wings of a gull,
as the olive believes it is filled with light,
and its oil will someday grace a god's tongue,
as my arms flail outwards and strike my forehead
in belief of a vestigial prayer process,
and I believe to allow them such historical pleasure
is hardly harmless from time to time,
as the transistor radio hears the woman
muttering and believes she requests
she be buried in the front yard with only her knitting
far from her husband the master of stratagems,
and weeping daughters once believed
their father had coated each grassblade with poison
and woke one morning to some twigs on the lawn
to believe they were dead starlings,
as the mountain believed it could stay hollow
long enough to return the tunnellers home,
and their wives believed in trying to believe
that rumble through clear skies was thunder,
I believe that is not what you wanted,
for you are only a guardian
geared to one particular moment
conjectured in no saintly book of apocrypha
when slowly at last the trucks will pull

into a warehouse shot through with shadows
and wherever I am I will see candles floating
on the ritual arms of two dark canals
and you will allow me to step I believe
into the mechanism
and tear off your wings

SOMETIMES LEAVING

Throughout the era of the tiny blemish
to the left of her eyebrow
I wandered clumsy
as a high school in late afternoon,
locked around glowing
cylinders of dust,
construction paper logic,
echoes of correct answers suppressed.
Sometimes leaving
a room can snap
your heart like a limb,
and not because there's anything in it.
For them, my seascape
of dresses impervious
and young careless hiding
search for care under brims,
I revealed behind my lecture on refusal,
but never myself
believed myself saying
lips live best
among the slow drape of hair,
especially raven.
Time of winter
like correspondence delayed
I did not yet remember
how on the counter your hands would sleep
unessential as summer,
while overhead the churning
silver impossible
winged
away and away from description
surveying our impasse

with one eye pretending
the other's not glass,
the car stolen and returned
unnoticed except for the jangle
of hey those aren't my glasses,
the pleasure
of the utterly faked confession,
or the intimate public
pleasure of glances
down the eyes of young mothers.
The eyes of young mothers
sleepwalk
clutching a hairbrush.
So many times I hypothesized
you actually standing
before this painting
of blue time choosing
at last from wherever
into my foot.
And I'm glad to have it.
It was probably lonelier than me.
I swear I won't doctor you,
or make you better, or even good.
You can contact your friends
if you have them
in whatever manner,
maybe radiating.

BLUEPRINT

I fumble downstairs like some old early riser
who has just dreamed of mowing the lawn with his cane.
One glass, some water and a tea bag
may be the forgotten alchemy of destruction.
The sea has withdrawn from the kitchen,
leaving one small whale which moans on the floor.
Spiders congregate on the dark wall, whispering
Have you heard about the insomniac dyslexic atheist?
The children's book who went to the marriage counselor?
The olive stuck on a desert island with a fan?
Alas, what is forbidden?
The sun rose while I was pouring.
I must have hit the switch.
Tomorrow, the dew will be a little colder,
and a few more leaves will creep through the mail slot.

The sun is a good conversationalist, if a little relentless,
and inclined to peer into my desk drawer, but it knows
the appropriate moment to go feed the morning glories.
I've laid out a compass, the porcelain boxes,
some colored chalk, a few photographs
of diving birds, and an atlas of mineral behavior.
Look, here's the future of Asia Major.
There are several rivers in need of a washing.
See what happens
after forty years of moonlight?
No eclipses until my thumb stops this talking.
After zero and equal there were thoughts.
All I had to do was create the world.
How I wish I didn't know what endless preparations
go on in that houseboat
beached at the end of the cul-de-sac.
For a long time I have felt a cloud in my pocket,
where I keep a promise, but I don't know why.

BEFORE THE POEM

Morning plays a fine false tune in the crook of the tree.
I get up to dance, I sit down.
Each leaf is a possible ending.
Great events are taking place in the house across the street.
Four actors rehearse a play I have written and left on their threshold.
Their shadows move from window to window, disappearing and reappearing.
I could shrink the world into a clouded watchglass, this is proven.

No matter which way I swivel my head,
there is light on the edge of the teacup.

I turn back
from a great abyss.

MIND THE GAP

A little portrait of me lies in the flowerbed,
making allusions, watching her comb her hair.
She sings into the shattered mirror:
"But you will last as long as the rose,
as long as the glass, glass tulips…"
A can opener smiles on the night table.

I remember she loved and feared the dark.
Whenever the horses broke loose
her heart trembled under my hand like a bat.
We'd huddle all night in bed, counting.
The horses filled us with the ineffable grandeur
of their silent pounding, or something like that.
Mostly I liked not knowing what to expect.

The sun looms angrily, high above, stranded.
She walks, or rather meanders towards my portrait chanting
"Phillip, your green thumbs, the envy of All Wales."
Each wisp of her hair grows larger, they wave and shine
like snakes you can see through. How strange. She bends
over me, blocking the sun.

VIEW ONTO THE BALCONY

The conductor shuffles his scores in the din
as the orchestra conjures and tunes.

A boatman stares down at the water. Reflected,
a few gulls cry and draw the name of a place.

Chin to her chest, she wears a slumped necklace of bone.
The rest of space hangs a blue cape on her shoulders.

She rocks, half in the boat and half in her chair.
The orchestra clatters to one long roaring tone,

dying out into the cavern which stands
silent before the great action.

We rise and applaud, madly, the musicians puzzled,
ready to begin their obliteration.

The auditorium is quiet again, except for wind
opening a glass door onto the balcony.

Two pigeons keep their eggs hidden in a pile of droppings and feathers.
Dark hills in the background rise up over the black railing.

Who will hear moss creep down the slope
over the child's knucklebone lost in the grass?

The music, as quiet as it was, could only begin to fill up the hall
with the name we forget, already perfect beyond recognition.

SUMMER CAMP

The day is wearing a white lab coat.
It is experimenting on us,
which is funny until you stop thinking about it.
Today I am going to drive my car
up into the mountain of distraction
where with my cat, Helix, I shall picnic.
Towards him I feel only slightly parental.
Only enough to feed him tiny
slivers of moral instruction
which he devours daintily without blinking.
Helix doesn't have a twin.
He is grey, and his left front paw
hurts him, though he has never spoken of it.
Past the blankness of his irises
is a lake of sadness, from which he was torn
many months ago, his mouth and tongue
frozen in a repetition of searching.
His mother was a sofa, a whole
neighborhood of comfort, support,
understanding, doors left unlocked,
kick the can, let's leave the neighbors
with the kids without even
formally informing them and drive
a car of distraction along the vanished town
of Calico up into the mountains
where we shall picnic. His father
was a cloud, as are all the fathers
of cats. Try to find one. The trail leads
through wet grasses down
to the culvert where I taught
myself to smoke like a wet idea
from which I have just withdrawn,

leaving only the tenderness.
There was a girl named Holly.
We knew each other in the park.
We were pineys.

PARK SLOPE

Where far into evening
speculation is
without further instruction
a staircase one kneels,
an always continuing upwards.
Where I inspect myself
for a black and white cat
who hides my sluggishness from inspectors.
His name is Joselito.
Where sometimes a word can fill the sails.
Where I grow smaller
like a view of a harbor.
Where hydrants are painted
hyacinths arguing
point with pleasure in every direction!
glitter slowly
through conversation with windows!
Where into the bitter dust of my mouth
I bring my face,
to stare back at tacit approval,
wearing huge red feverish hands
rubbing my beard
like a saint.
Where one logician
with half an eyeglass proposes
o perpetual attitudes of summer!
light grey sky
constitutes interference
and is proof of a wariness high above clouds.
Where his neighbor
pissing on the low wall contends
it was merely stolen

from thousands of silvery windows
by an amnesiac painter
a jump rope and naked laughter.
Where a silent chorus of blinking sirens
asks if so who forgot us
stretching it onto his scaffold?
Where down at the corner
of afternoon and 4th
children have been invented again.
Mischievous mothers
paroled from daytime
bend among the lounging bodegas,
filling their starry
implications of sundresses,
climbing a few rungs
of spanish without me.

A COLOSSAL HISTORICAL BLUNDER

Who gave the reasonable the right to name things?
Just the other day I was walking down the street
and got named. Just like that.
To be fair, it was unintentional.
She did it out of the corner of her eye,
accidentally. She was exceptionally matronly.
She toted a child whose eye twitched
whenever she looked away.
Powder-blue in polyester, on her way to work like a cloud.
As I said, I was walking down the street
minding everyone's business when
"semi-radical Jew with bad posture"
hit me like a brick between the eyes.
I unscrewed my face and tried
to give it back to her, but she said,
"No. Where would I hang it? Besides,
you read that in a book by Witold Gombrowicz.
Come back when you have something
less riveting to say."

SEPTEMBER FIRST

When I believed I had finally travelled
as far as a head
grim jew elves built through the air
could sail me,
I climbed down the ladder
bandaged in fog
and waited to be awoken.
It was enough to say
great barge skull
drift off into mist
trailing your ropes
my future asleep in your cargo
for the 22 Fillmore
to pass me
allowing my body to ride it
down to the La Bohème,
where a golem can drink
the pleasure of being
no one through a sugarcube,
finger the spines
of old russian paperbacks glued to the shelves,
and wait for short bouts
of backgammon with the Iranian's daughter.
Thus a whole year
with no dreams passed me
a smudge on a window
until my limbs
found a dead mouse scratching
forgive no one
in the dust.
He was entirely like
a toy neglect

had devoted to flatten.
I carried him
back down black iron steps
to recite in a park
named for escaping
whatever prayers were left.
Then to return, too soon, to find light
making tender
epiphany to the kettle.
For the matchmaker knows
like a beloved room
each thing must darken
all the wrong moments.
I know the perfect place for you.
A giant steel cavern
with sculptures of dust
that would surely disturb
the sleep of a Chinese governor.

I see you already
there in the shadows
shifting your many bodies,
crosslegged above the bodega
that never would close
feeding my naked fingers.
There are days that end
and there will be days
for escaping
the piano key
struck idly halfway across the city.
Whole days just for that sound
to drift
through chink after chink
in the tumult
and step through our window
wearing a cape of twilight.

THE INVISIBLE CITY OF KITEZH

Long before terrible hoofbeats approach,
it follows its bells into fog,
and marauders find only a gate of leaves

to slash with their pure hearts.
Every inhabitant goes on sweeping,
as if listening were not the only profession.

Except for climbing the stone tower
one at times wishes to burn,
along with the memory of dark hair

down the pure cliff of her shoulders,
the girl from the next town over
who whirled

into a black pile of ashes and boards.
Or is she still standing,
as we see her, growing older,

blurred in a vestment of snow,
paying tribute to the Gold Horde of seasons?
Like a smooth stone cradled in hand

for a moment then tossed back into the trees,
like a melody that follows
a blind princess into the birches,

is the invisible city.
You will see a belltower rise through trees
if you walk on, without your companions.

THE PATH TO THE ORCHARD

I once was afraid of everything living.
Then I put down that old wound

and began to follow
nevertheless like a shade through the trees.

How I died then waiting in frost.
I narrowed like a great ship's wake

with all my windows glinting behind me.
The apples were falling.

A sky full of white blossoms
broke on the stones of the orchard.

I smelled sweet pungent wine.
I saw one last inflamed glorious sun

returning to set on our backs.
I came closer and birds shook the branches

and screamed then grew sharp-eyed.
I could hear the unloaders laughing.

Back down the hill they carried baskets
of leaves burning in their arms.

Their eyes were angry.
I had found the path to the orchard.

CODA

1

Forever it seems they have gathered
each night at the house of the piano of course
to play until curfew and sometimes beyond

with no intent but to clamber like mice
along six notes of a melody
until
long after the cars from the opera
have passed under the window

they relax their hands
and fall asleep
one by one in their chairs

2

Rosa reads the lights in her necklace
while the drummer sits savagely eating an apple

no one believes him to be an informer
only in love

each morning he stomps along Great Arch Street
cutting through a courtyard littered with feathers

where a woman in a brassiere
is always hanging her laundry

he labors for hours in blocky notation
to copy last night's innovations

charting their path to some resolution

sleeps all afternoon
then goes to the bar at Hotel Inter-National

to place a grey envelope
in the hand of the statue of Glinka

3

Rosa
descends from a line
famous wherever women may play

no instrument but the voice

the one that she flashes
about herself

lightly

a master of swords

4

At first with a tempo
that always matches
intermittent rain

or maybe the blasts
of some night construction

they begin together
then each takes a turn
riding the melody
turning its head

performing some tricks

wandering so far
they can only be led back
gently at last
by the pianist's patient right hand

5

Tonight the samovar
with the patched hole
whistles on the table

there are almonds
and arabian coffee
meaning stay up late
someone is coming
his arrival will be
both bitter and sweet   −25−

6

Almost at dawn

three new notes emerge
from the battered guitar

and all fall silent

except for Rosa

7

who sings:

a blue banner
hisses through trees

a bird betrays the hidden city

the mouth of a factory
invites all crippled workers

two lovers grapple
next to a kettle

horses break their hooves
through government windows

and the fists which are now
pounding on our door

are also a kind of music

THE BOOK OF LEAVES

Long night filled with boxes of
of sparrows locked in hallucination

I'm sorry to wear you

like a cape
of daguerrotypes

I'm sorry I'm proud
of my steps
nailing this shack
to the quiet

and over the talking boulevards

clouds

catching a little sunlight in the shuteye

joke to clouds

the dogwood dies
of thinking
thinking makes a tree rotten

inside with desire

we keep always turned to the grass

when the grass
sings a semi-original tune

when clothes go bounding off the line

in a tumult
of red white almond and wind
to report to their lieutenant

their lieutenant the meadow

ordered to assemble a great conscription
of peacetime

colors

by blind rabbits of bureaucracy

by children slowly eating their smiles

(face lost over a table with streetlight)

we keep our body
always turned

to the sea silver temple rooftop of abstractions

this book was made for sequence

in the trees this book

of one of those mornings

someone has filled

the watering can with lilies

the lilies
I've been meaning

I've been for a long time floating
and floating on the afterwards surface

of that cabal of hieroglyphs devoted
to stories girls tell
when in love with their hats

my future always walking

a street in its pocket

with white hair I once mistook

it was just weakness in the dark

Now I blow smoke

now I blow into

my small blue book
full of no longer daydreams

and the thousand
arms of a sugar maple that loves me

CUPOLA

Clear solution
seeping from my nails

in Russia I ate
your coagulation.

Mushrooms a soldier's
mother sent him.

My hands in the jar
he watched

them crawl
until I was hungry

for uncaring.
Blue window

use me to see
the forest streaked

with blood and him
for innocence

searching.
Periodically rising

to wipe with Pravda
those nights

could have used
deutschmarks, it was all the same.

Tiny blind eskimos
cut off the underground,

no explanation
shot me forward,

my face got full, it wasn't
keeping, it flapped,

I was losing
an election

I drank solution
to dissolve

connective
tissue there were

no Chagalls, just billions
of motes, who burst,

my cells were damaged,
I sat on the first

green bench I found
and started

destroying
everything secretly.

LEAN TO

I was empty
and writing in the book you gave me

when that ten A.M. birdfeeder skylight
perfectly lifted

from morning hour
halted a moment beyond my fingertips

to perch half still
and three quarters in motion

a sketch of a hummingbird
by the blind artist from birth

an afterthought
ending June's longing for usefulness

Usefulness seemed
to be longing to be bound

in grateful pajamas
for once not running

after those truant watercolor hills
the TV has taken

the TV has taken
what is not now into

an irreparable darkening of tubes
Like an elder

dozing back into his boyhood
this hour

has paused once again
in my at last

my treehouse
Pulling it down

it could almost rest
for once in my perfectly

diminished palm
not thinking too hard

of the picture that caught
your eyes so full of leaves

the last of my missing my trouble of you   —33—

THE BLUE LIGHTS

Once, I followed them into a room I pried open

I asked the four shuddering hangers
I asked the painting of what was stolen from the pillow
I asked the wings hung from the windows
I asked the crowbar, the nails, the alphabet of dust

Have you seen them?

A bed not zoned for sleep
kept dreaming of forests

I asked the bar at the foot of the bed
What were you built to prevent?
Do you have an occupation for me?

The bar glowed, a little

I have no occupation
There is one city block I am devoted to knowing
Then a campus named by a crippled industrialist
Then a shed filled with cue balls

Then a river with speculated bridges
Then mountains sketched lightly in pencil

Then that which lies
illumined beyond
the plain beyond the mountains

A wooden table, and its lamp which sheds

the blue lights
and their instructions

TIBURON

How sweet to lie just once like a painter,
propped at the top of that hill on my elbow
considering the conundrum of breath.

Grasses blow among my limbs
as if wisdom had been withdrawn
for safekeeping into the library of fragments.

I have no purpose except to return
back down towards a eucalyptus I love.
Its petals are filled with the terrible weight

of careless reversal, grief without consequence.
It burns with such ease.
Just to stand there below it, dreaming of union,

all trembling and scent and colors of the moment,
is like living inside a flower
while making a study of winter.

Blue span that leads to a gleaming city,
you cannot be crossed by longing.

THE BOOK OF PAINTINGS

Dear blossom dearie
just now the announcer
missed the hour by an hour,
and the scratched coronets
of your early recordings
stumbled back into us.
By that missed hour
unnoticed
we did not get up naked
and call him a friend
to summer.
I remember you gave
yourself a blue dress
of not kissing.
You were off
somewhere beautiful
in the same way balancing
a lemonade as she sings
don't kiss me
yet kiss me again.
We all remember
with limbs colored
as a breeze through curtains
you're an expressionist
full of rectangular nudes,
you have in your eyes
no absolute bookshelves
filled with alphabetical books
of paintings
all sleeping
when you're not sleeping.
Yesterday you won't
be angry with me

in your blue dress
that fits me best,
my remembering.

NEW HAVEN

No caress is entirely unmechanical.
Days are never getting any longer.

Thus I am cracked, terribly,
as if a moon had crashed

into a steeple chuckling in darkness.
Archaically I wander

the forest of academic buildings
night and I have made huge

towards the lamp that glows on my desk,
frail as something imagined.

A RETURN

My hair is white.
So the journey was long.

I must have visited many ports.

Or just one,
where I stayed a long time
forgetting my language.

I bring you no fine scraps of cloth
in my empty hands.

And this bird on my shoulder
who remembers your name.

SCHOOL STREET

My house is so small
I bang my head
just thinking about it.

The house is old,
and "structurally unsound."
If you smoke inside

all the paint peels off
and the walls
fall down.

I sleep
in the refrigerator
with my feet sticking out,

I'm not sure why.
Somehow
the entire house

manages to face north.
A mad dog paces the attic
and howls

until I give him my dinner.
The backyard
is full of vipers.

The front yard
is an interstate.
To walk out that door

is suicide.
I'm plagued
by the demons of loneliness.

They mix my metaphors,
then brew me
a hellish soup.

The demons of loneliness
sit on my chest
and play with my navel,

leaving me
bruised and out of breath.
They are being punished too.

One of them even said,
"Like you
we are affected

by the cold the noise
and the wretched ceilings,
but the worst

is your endless complaining."
A man came to read the meter,
but he died

of a heart attack.
So they sent another man,
but he died

of one too.
Finally they sent
an archangel.

He lives next door.
All day he practices
sign language

into a mirror,
flexing his wings.
I know

he is there,
staring into his world,
keeping me

awake
with his silent
folktales.

WHAT EXISTS

Once, two rabbits slept in a basket.
One was born with six silver teeth.
The other had fur made of needles lost

when young mothers crossed a particular bridge.
Sometimes in sleep the smaller one bit.
Sometimes the larger one yawned,

and out poured a stone bell clanging,
black smoke sweeping over a flagstone,
tetrahedronal ruins.

The straw in the basket was golden
as the hair of a Botticelli,
one that slept for five hundred years

in a box in the palazzo de Medici cellar.
One I fell in love with when I was a child
playing marbles in chiaroscuro.

For a long time I knew who gave me the basket,
and I held it, standing next to a wall
surrounding an endless battle.

Now only my right hand exists,
stretched into the garden,
drenched at times by a rain

composed of tears from him who carved me.
My fingers are known among the deer
as the forest of wooden souls.

A HISTORY OF PETERSBURG

The scrape of two pairs of wooden skis
brings twilight down on the silver and spotted birches.

A path falls into darkness. She takes a wrong turn
into the thrill of returning alone.

Just a few hours, he whispers, until
fur coats heaped on the sofa, the piano coming closer.

A dried orange peel is carried from room to room.
The carriage rattles home along the icy embankment.

The lock turns, a comb
rests on the floor by silk slippers.

We will always savor her like a glance
held a fraction too long across a theater.

Like a dream conversing in a quiet novel.
Like a cry kept safe in a wooden drawer,

a diagnosis scrawled on blue notepaper,
gunfire, convalescence, the brush of a glove.

THE HOUSE ACROSS THE WATER

Today I awoke before my desire.

At the foot of the bed
it lay in its sore spot,
twitching in nightmare or dream.

I passed my hand over it,
like an abscess.

In the quiet I dressed
and once again walked down the hillside,
to crouch in the snow
by the water.

No birds were aware of me.
They came and went,
nothing resembled anything else.

The house across the water was still,
as if it would always be frozen.

NOT ME, NOT YOU

He is trapped at the end of the short age of the typewriter.
A black flower blooms in his chest.

Like two armies shifting from foot to foot,
she kneels tending hers

in the dirt of her restless garden.
The trees are no longer

wondering contraptions.
Men wearing hoods,

they fix her in silver daguerre.
World, black circle, die of contrivance.

On Elba his boots
the pale Bovaries say

once tramped through her hair,
slowly dodging

sun in the parlor without her.
His circle of friends lifts him onto a chair.

Men in the trees.
She wishes to wish without contrivance.

Why are these implements so unerotic?
Because your first lieutenant,

a husband of some crocus willing
to let him shrink from your touch,

ages through peacetime.
Because the eighth planet

has just been captured,
and can tell the past.

Because you are about to discover
once and for all but not before

a long orgasm to kill
the urge for a quick solution.

A century later he still can't believe
they titter at illicit touches.

He wanted so much to kiss
the advent of movies.

In a bar he reached out unthinking
and lit her cigarette. They threw him

out on his ear, which bled for days.
Into the gauzy and waiting

she walks, her vanity shines,
the mirror a novel

of rooms in revolution
he will someday lift

in an attic, so like the smoldering
greengrocer's assistant

she glimpsed one town over,
resentfully stacking crates.

Because they were meant for each other
they will never meet, not even here.

She flowers with ease
in her room of perfumed breezes.

He falls asleep in her bed, his face covered in pages,
dreaming the word candelabra.

SPRING

All through the ritual flutter of hands   you pretended to conjure
it stood there outside you   many years   stillborn   over and over
though you nursed it   composed   always its blue lips   remembering
those chars in the pit   now buried in infinite grass   the white mountains
waiting outside   I know   the precept of shadows   even touching your hair
remember   touching them all   you somehow went on

KICK THE CAN

The last thing on my mind was tragedy
when I wandered into the sun-stippled battlefield
of the little town known as breakfast.

First was that platonic cup of coffee hovering
one inch above my allotted formica portion
for me to grasp like a new method.

The town is usually torn in a productive balance
swinging between up in the one hand
a tiny disproportionate exertion of gravity gleaming

dully on the hill like a college, and down
in the valley of the other a diffuse clumble
of concrete structures through which stride

prophets of thunder and abstraction
mumbling into the clocks in their beards.
And the swamp someone sold us

as farmland between them.
But today a summer has been declared,
so the newspaper on my doorstep

is blank unconditional silence.
Except for the item of how I'm forgetting
the death of my love

for a pale and southern song of songs,
she who was once a pitcher of milk
on a hillside below a proverbial scumble of clouds,

she who pulling the dress
of the simple pleasure of making
tightly round her like a pastoral dream,

lazily drew with her fingers in grass
a map of how close to approach a love,
she who at times would release her breasts

to tumble confused and newly-awakened
like rabbits into the meadow of my sight,
where they would right themselves,

often gloriously. Upon them for hours
she let me rest my head, especially
when thinking of something else.

ARCADIA

The meadow is not too flat, with a scarecrow in a wedding dress, a ruined barn, and a stream that catches light mechanically. A woman bends over it, turning her limbs, always looking down to see how beautiful she is as a linden.

Hidden in her branches a magpie stares, as if summer had suddenly ended, listening to a shadow approaching from the south, while bees who had been sleeping curled in twos and threes inside the cups of snowdrops grow frantic, trying to burst out of their prisons.

Slowly the Floating Amusement Park interposes itself between meadow and sun, while the linden grows flushed, turning her leaves towards the whirling lights and claxons, and the stream twists in an agony of bliss.

Phrases begin to rain down. Who was it again who said it is always the same question? Even a grassblade thinks. Did I truly get what I deserve? More and more, so many it's like static in the hall of angels before the meeting is called to order.

Before we can ask how long, it is suddenly gone. Not far off a little bell is ringing around the neck of a cow. If you lay a hand between his ears, he will raise his head to meet it, still grazing, and you will know he used to be a soldier.

THE BOOK OF OAKLAND

Sarah I never got to show you
the while you were leaving between us

and its table covered with versions
of continuing plastic flowers

once watered by laughter and choosing
(how is it now they are wilting)

or the shelves I fell down for an hour
lifting my eyes and handing them

to the student of normal psychology
who came to sit in your chair

and left with Logic
in his briefcase meowing

among a few signed scraps of regret
or what at last blossomed

instead of spring in the lot
across from our bed and its favorite

white widening into
and how I never was seasick

except on the sea
and never again while falling

FRIENDS OF OLIVIA

Between the widow and the bride
erupts a long misunderstanding
on which we sit sipping our Max
Amadeus von Dopplegangers.
That is to say cups of clear personal plastic
in which our reflections furiously myriad
oval black pools of resentment.
The widow erupts from the floor.
She wants us to say to ourselves,
children, you must be punished, but not
at the moment, for there are all sorts
of people sleepwalking around
doing grieving things like ordering
ghost orchids from catalogs,
and arranging for great eulogies
to be slipped under overcoats.
You must be punished for the use of certain
greek constructions allowing
for laziness of thinking, pandering,
jealousy, derivation, and all the other
etceteras compiled
by a classic breeze
through which tagalog tanktops toss themselves
like another view of a certain
partially placid espresso drink
unlikely to pluck harshly your strands
or promote the sort of productive
meditation on lust that sends you
dizzily through the endless
shooting towards the library.
But not at the moment, which belongs
as always to the bride, more unfinished

than the essay on repetition,
which she so unassumingly adores
that we may continue
to employ it for merits we can just
plain old trust. She is a sculpture
reaching for a skylight to obliterate
her white distance from us.
I am a sail driven by a well-
meant yet partially foul exhaling
from the widow. There is someone
I so terribly want towards.
The slightest shift in a sunbeam traversing
the studio of her face
levers in me a great wonderment.
I wonder what would the pleasure
of winter do. Could I survive
all that brief kissing
under the unplanned panoply
of couches and mandarin oranges?
The face of the bride, white, multiple,
oval, is no cleavage from us.
She knows the language of afternoons.
She knows the language
of the room with coats where one deposits
missed kisses before emerging
out into the gleaming
I'm too shy to mention
even to you. Between the widow
and the bride blazes a slow
generative misunderstanding.
Whole hours I will wonder
where you are, door in a dream,
raven haired I owe you nothing,
moon I carry around in my pocket
like half a pair

of spectacles abandoned.
Somewhere inside me I've hidden
the switch. I am guilty
of countless secret constellations.
Through the gallery I drag my breath
made famous for danger
by a radio that cannot stop chattering
how it has eaten
the final chrysanthemum.
Only the library of my hands
with its black windows remembers
that when you were gliding
up and down the elm lined street
under your hand like a bicycle
named for the briefest phase of spring,
though you seemed so lonely for always.

THESE WINDOWS

I opened my eyes like a leaf blown gently from sleep. I could see a few trees already contentedly moving their limbs, while wasps softly hammered the large glass pane. In the garden, a man was seated in a white lawn chair, his face buried in a newspaper, his fine black bowler peering and nodding. For many nights he and I had huddled over a scarred black mahogany table, returning at times to opposite corners to stare at the sheet blemished by only a few black figures floating between us and like us awaiting. Beside me a woman was dozing, wearing a purple veil. Just then I heard someone named Iris warn me with a laugh from the past that such an obscurement would be the fashion this spring, so I should not feel disappointed, or frightened, or lost in a landscape of customs into which I had stumbled or drifted. At such moments she turned her head sideways and laughed, and I heard something fall and shatter from the height of childhood or clouds. Lifting the veil, I revealed the oval mirror where her face had been, and reaching a hand into my reflection, so as not to frighten them carefully closed these windows.

–57–

WARNING: SAD

The day has a light concussion.
A droplet,
down its grey stoic thread of rain
I dangle
into the museum of trees.
The trees keep asking for change,
and I am trying, desperately,
to take them literally
where spring isn't a moment late.
I am dressed like a giant rabbit
only I can see.
Hopping thunderously
I carry a basket
of occurences some smallish person thinks
are colored promises, and hates me

for pushing
her hands from Easter.
Now rain has shut
and an hour sneezes
remembering a wall of photographs
I had built of myself
as if I were
by way of reminding.
It then occured to me,
it being there must be a syndrome
in which happiness is a disease preventing
others from being thought of
harmlessly, even playfully.
How utterly
I am unlike
a drink in a museum with a glance
a la Balanchine.

Through everything during parties
a talky thread dangles,
unifying like pouring a drink,
but I am but next to your window
a wooden staircase
up and down which your neighbors
cannot seem to remember
not to run.
If I say I into your place of work
today will dangle
four times through my shirt to make you laugh
you will know my way
of saying inside my chest
I have a nothing
composed of I stumbled
into your place of work today
and made love
to my idea of you carelessly.
Will you hand me
the other half
of what then will I be
with you no longer a mystery?
Great syntactical hunger,
I am a lunch poem
in which with you or at all
when I'm not spending it
time hurts at noon.

THE BOOK OF THE OLD WORLD

A woman made happy by nothing at twilight,
a blue and white kerchief on her head.

The road she walks on winds itself
through a map fallen from your hands.

You have lost your chance to be sad for a reason.
You say does it matter.

No one controls her footsteps.
The villagers no longer gather apples

only to turn into blossoms and drift
down Ragged Hill onto the lake.

Still she will pause at the edge
and bunching her skirts in her fist

reveal a white flash of ankles
just as her grandmother told her never to do.

The lord of desire lives in a poplar.
He'll turn you into a flock of swallows.

In the last glow from the top of the hill
she bends down to dry her feet with her hair.

When she rises, her skirts fall over her ankles
like grey cloth over a dovecote.

She hurries off towards some lights in the distance.
Good night, go into your story in peace.

DO YOU REMEMBER

When we were children behind the church
there was an enemy coming on always from over the pond
we parcelled out salaries of pebbles
we were always dividing
the gravestones had to be kept alone
and the sacks of potatoes
they look so much larger now under the Polish signs
were the bodies that rose up at night and leapt onto the swings
to continue our work
do you remember I did not know you
though each day we met behind the church
it did not belong to me
truckdrivers thumbs up horns and cigarettes
always knew us
they were part of the larger battle
our raging discussions of which way the weathervane pointed
when it meant rain
and what signal we would be given
when it was time to lay down our branches

SCARECROW

Remember her strapped to the air,
her grey dress flapping a little?

The field mice ran beneath her feet
learning new technologies.

I don't scare anybody, she complained,
smiling, a nest on her head.

Which was how much I loved her,
all through the harvest
and dismantling.

I am the morning dove
who nests in the gutter.

I am singing sadly to the barn.

THE BOOK OF WAVES

I try to be a good hillside,
my eyesight salty and clear,
and hold still all night.

Below me the now-darkened meadow
watches over its sails in the harbor.
I remember between one life and another

my two friends and I made a third
in the meadow. Like three fenceposts,
the plot we encircled was small.

Inside a calf slicked down by rain
watched us believe
we were building a barn in her eyes.

A few cries escaped from our mouths,
returning to settle like clouds of sparrows
onto our wooden bodies, turning us back

into something a bit less mournful.
Then we were bent over the atlas.
And our fingers chose of their own accord.

Tonight inside the house on my back
my two friends are together again.
She sits twirling a moment onto her finger,

as if she can hardly accept its proposal.
He stands at his post at the window.
By now, they have grown so tired.

Soon the room they creep into will know
how easily those no longer lovers lie
in the cat's cradle of knitted afghans.

All the next hours will be empty shelves.
Until I'm a storm,
and only a flower knows me.

AMERICAN LINDEN

When you'd like to remember the notion of days,
turn to the barn

asleep on its hill,
a red shoulder holding the weight of clouds.

You could stand still for so many moments.
So little is over and over required,

letting the wind brush your crown.
The lathes of tobacco swing into autumn.

Swallows already discuss the winter.
I know you are tired of imagination.

All that clumsily grasping the sunlight.
Aren't you tired of bodies too?

Whenever it rains, they fall from the sky
and darken your window.

Clutching each other they call out names
while you sit in the circle thrown by a lamp

and pretend they are leaves.
The potatoes cringe and bury their heads.

Do you see them?
They know where to return when hoofbeats come.

Like you they were not born with pride,
they were born with skins made of earth.

Their eyes are black, and they sing out of tune,
quietly, under the snow.

THE BOOK OF THE BROKEN WINDOW

Lost face laden with streetlight

you and I have been in the book

trying to touch each other and leave

stars in the lake

where we do not belong

evening in the street

where we many times were

I am done with mine own personal anthology

of tin roof morse in the rain I believed

was holy transmitting nothing

I am done turning

the barge of midwinter days towards snow

stars are never angry regarding

what gets to be beautiful?

I have seen a man

placing water in cups

for pigeons who bring

afternoon to his shoulders

So much concerned green hum

I have seen

electricity a gathering hand

from the apartments

from the apartments it must be deflected

with promises emptied

I have seen past the cars

munching their idea of green

like what I call money

past the body

cannot be so easily fooled

the apartments lower their eyebrows

at the street before a girl's face is darkened

like roses lunge out of the baby's breath

and lighten a girl's face with blood

I hear them coming

the two-bit madrigal of the radiator

the pious absence

bells tumble annoying at intervals hidden

the urban church of consonant mutes

loading in things as I with my brother

once loaded squares of hay

the forgotten months

when only a few words

are still useless moving

from hand by spain distracted

to a postcard of shields

crying into the rubble

of light a museum and etc.

rubble of the breeze

and its slow march upwards

to shit covered spires

where its masks await

I AM A SCULPTOR

Although I have never once seen one half of the angel
emerge into altered air
while the other sleeps senselessly
folded still in a block of stone
I have come more and more each day to resemble
as it lies there against a wall tormented
by my refusal to grant a caress
of the jeweled point I might drive an increment deeper
so gaze may wrestle there longer with darkness
nor have I relented only to see
the white lips of my past
converse with my past in a tumble
of limbs and the spaces without me between them
nor chosen a different path in anger
and placed a spotlight behind
one particular thought
I mangled and forced in a torn form of steel
throwing its shadow onto a wall
all the time knowing no man walks the earth
any longer with lamp and compassion
nor have I repented and wished to repair a wound
I choose to believe I have made in the earth
with a huge rusted suture
of towers and teeth that hunger
and hunger for meaning
still it is true that I have them
my fat disobedient monks
they have built me a temple again
from some insect wings filaments binding
the iridescence they could or would not
lift off the floor
they have once more filled the structure with doubt's breath

stolen from my lips as I slept and again
they shall wander condemned over my face for a term
of forty times forty finger years
crying out in their happy tumultuous chorus
we were only obeying the eye!
the eye that raises its inscrutable chisel
and burning and shouting
commands us to go out and wander and leave
untouched all the things
we could ever imagine it loves

TEN QUESTIONS FOR MONA

I'm sitting at the same table again, in the hopes.
This time I'm sitting where you were.
Like a fragrance you had stayed to rise,

having felt just long enough under your hat,
wanting exactly what you want.
Like a fragrance you had strayed.

There are masculine and feminine willows
moving about this room.
Just now tiny machines manufacture noises

devoting themselves to the removal
and the placing. Tiny machines
manufacture noises producing

in me a feeling of productivity.
Just now a shadow
approached from the west door spilling

a glance upon me, sorry, I thought
it was you sitting down in the place
where your hands shook as you poured

evening's sweet wine out in photographs.
I watched you grow older in the approach.
Summers are loose and feathery

in consequence as a high school, or a time,
or a camp in which Right Now is a time.
You say you think of it in a good way,

in the long approach, i.e. laughter
and lightness and etcetera time
of staying too long and leaving too soon,

sitting across from you, that absolute
conditional you sitting down in the place
where I had been a glance upon me.

Right Now is a time. A child needs
to be moved less fearfully
than thinking of something else.

What flower do you bring a flower?
I'd curl up in the wrist, but there's a cat
already named there for luck and howling.

What flower do you bring a trouble?
In the course of a sleeping farther away
dawn grew your hair.

I watched you grow younger.
When I look up you will be across from me.
This time I'm sitting where you were.

I HAVE A FRIEND

Into the black square of four o'clock
I exited, almost too catlike,
and a whole symphony
of climbing back in incorrectly
climbed back in your glowing
rose above me window.
Those are just two
of the several colors of silence
I thought had only one.
You initiate me into the first
before one thinks of speaking,
and the second that into public places
such as a restaurant we are holding
hands in descends periodically
untethered to events despite
what C. says astral or otherwise.
With a gesture composing the fourth you placed
the cassette with the third into my bag,
so during travels I could hear
always the needle
tracing that emptiness time
the gate of something gently to talk about
opened, and through it trickled
a tiny stream of wailing that's night
remembering a morning attitude
tears made parental.
I am still holding, thinking of where
no waves crash on a street
you use every day at my own risk.
Down it Ramona is learning to ride
two wheels into as if
there were no parents at all.

Sometimes a doorway passes her tracing
a chrysanthemum onto one of your drawings.
Sometimes she talks like a child
imitating one, until I regard her
until she crumbles back into a small adult
who knows already the book about
the books growing too large
for her little leopard backpack.
I'd give her one thousand afternoons of staring
into a white paper
not thinking of letters
arriving only when we think of them,
but she's already so beyond
that last instance of crawling between
our six in the mornings.
Sometimes I watch her swaying
totally unlike a tree.
Like a spring snow too much talking

stayed a while then melted,
leaving the trellis I am nailing
together with hurtling and always below you,
until on my lap you perch
wearing the dress of future photographs
from which you regard me.

SO BE IT

I was building a little version of you
from the few foreign coins
nails stray facts and keys
I had hauled along my peregrination
through others and furnished rooms.
Thus I saw in a YMCA
how you sat like Dustcloud
Arizona, composing me long
clarifying truth lines
passed like missives from hand
to dream, only a radio
made mostly of tin foil
the end of the hall is always borrowing,
an hombre with a broken mouth
and a pet fly named relic
or molybdenum to keep you
constant and wandering.
Or I see sometimes
you in the pool, staring at blue
gradual lengthening days
and ever more sentient mildew,
rising up with a wet hand to grasp
the number I once handed you
over a sort of bridge of beer and foaming.
So many such untethered visions
I pick up in a kind of abstract
awareness of ringing,
and it is you quite strangely
with whom in a light year
I have not spoken
calling from Connecticut,
a state based on convolution

and reticence to union.
For once I believe I am managing to sound
totally absolute and hollow
in the midpoint between
distance and feeling.
But it's just the snowstorm currently
sucker punching
our little jawbone of a town.
From my window I can see it
still sliding with a smile on every steeple
into a blissful three-day coma,
glad with white hair
on every thinking surface
to be old! at last! not a single future day
filled with an occupation of striving,
every moment from now a front porch
into which contemplation
strides in her sundress wearing
a perfume of extract once-removed.
And glad to hang up I continue
my conversation between
the me that was feeling secretly
and a little glad to feel
crummy and lie abed continuing
fully funded research into the me that prefers
sitcoms to any sort
of human or literary bliss,
and the me that pretty clearly gets
pleasure out of looking disapproving
into such evenings and their residents.

THE BOOK OF THE WRONG KIND OF BLUE

Sunday morning up early covered
    in a dream still fleeing
the slow premises of me,

a luxury of blue flowers
softly screaming

don't ever not spend
all day with her sketching
the dead pink bicycle

no matter how angry
    the trees that is to say
    the wind

that is to say
the blue
between us revoked when we looked at it.

I'm moving waterfalls
near you of blue
    that could hear us,
they are concerned.

Wrong kind of blue
    tried to embrace me,
but I was emerging

from how I could live
my way back into the neighborhood
of your name

with its green in their eyes
cats that hunt
my blue.

Your front porch
        extended
the next version of limbs

twined and improved by always lesser techniques
dawn uses
in recording us.

What are you refusing?

Your paintings have grown
deep red avenues
down which golems

carry
manuals
written by night

to maintain insomnia levels.

You move surely
through a door
emanation
blue with interior lab light.

Soon no one will be sleeping.

Just xeroxing xeroxes
until only gaps
are visible.

Like ones you already
send me
that send me

through morning so thick
with dreamless excuses
I once made for my head,

a deep pond

I sit beside considering
the finest blue way
not to write you.

Dear halter,

black sails of your scratched lp's
fill no longer
with resignation.

At the head of the stairs
a girl sits reading
her fingers surprised.

I came up to tell you

I have never seen
such beautiful scissors.